ROCKIN THE CLOUD INTERVIEW

The Ultimate Cloud Summary Cheatsheet

and Cloud Computing Primer

- The newest science behind the interview process
- Secrets to negotiating the best salary or contract rate
- Increase your technical acuity
- Understand Cloud terminology
- Short concise Cloud question and answer reference
- Get an understanding of Cloud Computing

Perfect for anyone who wants an understanding of what the Cloud entails without getting bogged down into low-level technical information. Pass your technical interview and get the job you deserve. This book is a must have for anyone in technology.

Greg Unger

Ordering Information

Quantity sales. Special discounts are available on quantity purchases by corporations, associations, and others. For details, contact us.

Orders by U.S. trade bookstores and wholesalers, please contact us.

Contact Information

Email address: businessathlete101@gmail.com

Website: http://www.thebestsellingbooks.org

Dedication

To you the reader. I write these books to pass on the knowledge I've gained over the years so you don't have to go through the trials and tribulations I went through.

Those who have a hard time remembering reference materials, this book is for you. I want you to succeed and I hope this book serves you well.

Hopefully this levels the playing field and gets you the job you deserve. If you're going so far as to prepare yourself by reading this book, then I know you deserve it.

Table of Contents

Chapter 1 Interview basics 1

Your attitude 1

Assess your skills and experiences 1

Create a list of relatable experiences 2

Practice relating the experiences aloud 2

Participate in mock interviews 4

Behavior based interviews 5

Themes for these types of questions include: 5

First impressions 6

Dress professionally for the position 7

Plan ahead to be on time 7

Introduce yourself politely to the receptionist 8

Greet the interviewer cordially 8

Expect small talk 8

The Interview 9

Points to Include in the Interview 9

More Tips 10

How will you be evaluated? 10

Refrain from reciting memorized answers 11

Maintain proper body language 12

Be prepared to ask questions 12

If the interview is not going smoothly, don't panic. 13

Expect the unexpected 13

The closing is important 14

Concluding the interview 14

Questions to consider asking at the close of the interview 14

Questions to avoid 15

The conclusion of the interview 15

Follow up 16

Chapter 2 How I got started 17

Chapter 3 The art of salary negotiation 25

Do your research 26

Talk money early 28

Some recruiters have WAY more latitude than they let on. 30

Believe that you CAN negotiate in this economy 34

Don't be afraid to ask — But don't demand, either 34

Keep selling yourself 35

Make them jealous 36

Ask for a fair price 36

Negotiate extras and be creative! 37

Be confident 37

Keep track of what you have done well 38

Don't take it personally 38

Chapter 4 How to become a remote worker 40

Chapter 5 Cloud Terminology 46

Chapter 6 Cloud Interview Questions 65

Chapter 7 Azure Interview Questions 85

Foreword

This book is broken up into sections by subject. You will find redundancy in some of the questions because they cross-pertain to multiple subjects. This makes it easier to skip to one subject or another without any cross-dependency. Some of the questions are simple while others are difficult. I'd suggest you know the answers to all questions even if you just memorize the answer. The answers are short and to the point. If you feel you're lacking understanding of either the question or the answer, I urge you to do further reading.

This is your profession and like any profession you must become a master. You must know the language inside and out to be the best you can be.

Don't worry if you need to re-read this book a few times. Most people will need to. I find it useful to follow-up when reading a book like this so I can review in practice things I learn while reading.

I tried to make this as comprehensive as possible without turning this into a reference guide. By no means is this book exhaustive. I could add another couple hundred pages and still not cover everything, given the topics I've included.

I don't provide you examples and samples to explain the answers. This question and answer reference is meant to get your mind to recall what you already know by giving you short, concise and easy to remember answers.

You'll find I don't group the questions in sections very often. I do this purposely to make your brain work harder in order to commit the information to memory.

Cloud Computing represents one of the most significant shifts in information technology many

of us are likely to see in our lifetimes. We are reaching the point where computing functions as a utility, promising innovations yet unimagined. The major roadblock to full adoption of Cloud Computing has been concern regarding the security and privacy of information.

Much work has been done regarding the security of the cloud and data within it, but until now, there have been no best practices to follow when developing or assessing security services in an elastic cloud model - a model that scales as client requirements change.

CHAPTER 1   INTERVIEW BASICS

Your attitude

Let me start out by saying that your attitude is going to possibly play the biggest role in whether or not you get a great job. Because of this, prepare to be in the right state of mind <u>before</u> you sit down in front of an interviewer. As with almost all things, everyone gets better with practice. To be a top contender for a job, there's nothing better than completing a successful interview. And interviews can be intimidating prospects. Here are some suggestions to help you prepare to present yourself at your best.

Assess your skills and experiences

• Focus on three to four areas where your skills are the strongest. Knowing these will help you tell your interviewer why they should hire you.

• Practice describing your special talents and skills.

• Examine your work and education background. Look for skills and experiences that match the job description.

Create a list of relatable experiences

Employers want real examples of how you behave professionally.

• Identify examples that relate to the job description and where you have performed well using your skills and background.

Practice relating the experiences aloud

• Organize your thoughts and communicate clearly.

• Explain the situation.

• Describe your role or task.

• Describe the action you took

• Describe the results cf your action.

• Include what you lecrned or what you might do differently in the future.

• Memorize your answers ahead of time but do NOT come off like the answers were memorized. No one wants to listen to a scripted, pre-recorded message but you also want to make sure you say the right thing.

Organizing your thoughts ahead of time and practicing them aloud will help you to feel more confident and communicate clearly in the interview. Be able to describe your useful skills in layman's terms in case your interviewer is not an expert in the field.

Example:

SITUATION: When I worked at the state library, many of the books were not filed correctly.

TASK: I was in charge of shelving books on three floors.

ACTION: I designed and proposed a new employee training method to my boss. I then presented the new method to the library assistants at the next staff meeting and everyone contributed ideas for the new training on shelving.

RESULT: After that meeting, there were fewer misplaced books, and customers asked fewer questions about finding missing books.

Participate in mock interviews

Practice the interview process to improve your communication and overcome nervousness and anxiety.

I'd go so far as to interview for jobs that I didn't even want, just to practice. You should be able to work on your demeanor and confidence level if you know, going into the interview, it isn't a job you want. Try new things and see what kind of response you get. When you don't have to worry about getting the job, you can focus on the fundamentals of being an interviewee.

Mock interviews will help you as well. You can do them with a friend or family member or in a mirror. You do whatever you have to do in order to get the job. This may sound like an odd thing to have to do but you won't think it odd when you get the job because you were prepared. Mock interviews help you get a feel for the interview process. They're also an opportunity to create a personality in your head that you can tap into whenever you're in this type of situation. Being a good interviewee is not about how smart you are, it's about how trained you are and how comfortable you are. Believe me when I tell you that your comfort level will increase exponentially, the more training you have. Practice verbalizing how your background, skills and abilities fit the job you are interviewing for.

Behavior based interviews

Behavioral based interviews and questions have become standard practice. Recruiters ask for detailed descriptions on how you handled yourself in certain tasks and situations. The premise is that past behavior predicts future performance.

Themes for these types of questions include:

• Disagreements and conflicts with coworkers

• Innovative solutions to problems

• Qualities of a team leader and qualities of a team member

• Meeting or failing to meet deadlines

• Responding to criticism from a superior, co-worker, or classmate

• Persuading someone to accept your idea or concept

• Seeing a problem as an opportunity

• Adapting to a wide variety of people, situations, and/or environments

First impressions

First impressions are lasting ones. Often, they are made during the application process, even before the interview starts.

• Voice messages may be the employer's first impression of you.

- The message on your answering machine or voice messaging should be courteous and professional.

- Inform everyone who might answer your telephone that employment calls may come at any time. If you feel your roommates or members of household are unreliable, consider listing cell phone number. Be sure to manage your cell phone calls appropriately.

• Any time you interact with a potential employer or anyone on their staff, imagine that they are evaluating you.

• Be respectful in the way you dress and the way you act.

• Be positive, upbeat and professional when corresponding in person, by mail, phone or email.

• The person answering your questions or taking your application may be the CEO sitting in for the receptionist on a break. You never know!

Dress professionally for the position

• Research industry expectations regarding attire. This could be simply walking through the lobby of the workplace to observe how employees dress.

• Being dressed a little more formally than your Interviewer is acceptable. It shows respect for them, the position, and the company.

• Get plenty of sleep the night before. Your physical appearance will be at its best when you are alert and rested.

• Avoid perfumes and cologne. Your spouse or significant other may think you smell great, but the person who interviews you may not.

Plan ahead to be on time

• Map your route to the interview site.

• Know where to park and how to enter the building. (Do you need a photo id for security?)

• Plan to arrive 10-15 minutes early.

Introduce yourself politely to the receptionist

• Introduce yourself to the receptionist and tell them the purpose of your visit along with your name.

• Thank the receptionist for their assistance.

• The receptionist is one of the first employees of the company you will meet. While receptionists may not be making hiring decisions, they may mention their impressions to the interviewer.

Greet the interviewer cordially

• Greet your interviewer using Mr., Ms. or Mrs.

• Shake their hand.

• Tell the interviewer your name.

• Wait to be offered a seat before sitting.

• Relax yourself to appear friendly and be memorable.

Expect small talk

• Engage in the conversation, be responsive and take initiative.

• Don't worry if the conversation catches you off guard, the interviewer may be testing you to see how you react under pressure. Try to relax and respond naturally.

Many interviewers will begin the interview with casual conversation. This is a prelude to the interview where they examine your responses for qualities the company seeks. One of the greatest things you can do for yourself is to come up with 5 questions to talk about before-hand. On top of that, come up with witty answers and responses that you can make to further the discussion. If this is practiced enough, your first impression will be a great one.

The Interview

Your goal in an interview is to show and tell your best qualities to the interviewer. Understand that the interviewer 's goal is to evaluate you on criteria other than just your skill.

Points to Include in the Interview

• How you fit the job qualifications

• Why you want the job

• Why you want to work for the organization

• What you can contribute to the employer

• What you have learned about yourself and your work

More Tips

• Relate your background and accomplishments to the employer's needs.

• Don't talk about what was wrong with past jobs or past employers.

• Be sincere, positive, and honest with your answers.

• Have your resume and/or portfolio with you in a professional looking folder.

• Avoid mentioning financial concerns or personal problems.

• Take notes during the interview. Make sure you write down everyone you speak to, dates, times and questions asked. This will make you look diligent and engaged and will allow you to reflect upon the interview afterwards. Do not however, ignore the interviewer in order to take notes. Short-hand works wonders here.

How will you be evaluated?

Once the official part of an interview begins, interviewers will carefully listen and evaluate your responses. In addition to your knowledge about the job and interaction styles, they may look for the following qualities:

• How well do you understand the job and meet its qualifications?

• What skills do you use when interacting with others?

• How mentally alert and responsible are you?

• Can you draw proper inferences and conclusions during the course of the interview?

• Do you demonstrate a degree of intellectual depth when communicating, or is your thinking shallow and lacking depth?

• Have you used good judgment and common sense regarding your life planning up to this point?

• What is your capacity for problem solving?

• How well do you respond to stress and pressure?

Refrain from reciting memorized answers

• Present yourself as interested and naturally enthusiastic about the job, not rehearsed and flat.

• Research the position and organization to fit your skills to the job.

- Formulate concise arswers.

Maintain proper body language.

- Sit up straight and lock alert.

- Avoid fidgeting.

- Smile when appropriate.

- Maintain eye contact when being asked questions.

- Be aware of your tone of voice. Keep it energetic and avoid monotone answers.

Body language says more about an individual than their words. Match your body language to the impression you want to make.

Be prepared to ask questions

- Prepare 3-5 questions ahead of time. Again, being prepared here will behoove you. You will most likely ask the exact same questions in every interview, so be prepared ahead of time. The more inquisitive you are; the more interest you show.

- Ask about the duties of the job early so you can target your answers to the position.

- Pay attention to an employer's body language and watch how they react to your questions.

• Some employers may start the interview by asking whether you have any questions. Others will tell you that they have set aside time at the end for questions. Still, others might be comfortable with you asking questions throughout the interview.

If the interview is not going smoothly, don't panic.

• Some interviewers might test you to see how you handle stress.

• Stay positive.

• Ask your interviewer to repeat anything you don't understand so you can gather your thoughts.

Expect the unexpected

Sometimes questions are asked simply to see how you react.

• Pause briefly.

• Consider the question.

• Give a natural response.

During the interview, you may be asked some unusual questions. Surprise questions could range from, "Where do you see yourself in 5 years" to "If you could live in any time period, which one would it be and why?"

When unexpected questions come up, take note of them either immediately or as soon as possible. If one person asked this question, chances are another might so be prepared with a witty answer next time.

The closing is important

Concluding the interview

• Remain enthusiastic and courteous.

• Ask questions.

• Prepare questions ahead of time to help you decide if the position is suitable for you.

• Leave the interviewer(s) with three things that you would like them to remember about you.

This is also an opportunity to give additional information about your background that you think is pertinent to the position and that was not covered in the interview.

Questions to consider asking at the close of the interview

• What do you want the person in this position to accomplish within the first three months?

• Are there are any important skills needed for the job that have not been covered in the interview?

• What is the time frame for making the hiring decision?

• What are the core working hours?

• Does the position require me to be on call?

• How big is the team I would be working with?

• Is the environment laid back or a bit more rigid?

• What is the dress code?

Questions to avoid

• What is the starting salary?

• What are the vacation related perks, company benefits, or other perks of the job?

Wait for the interviewer to introduce these subjects. The best time to talk about salary is after you have been offered the job. You're then in a much better position to negotiate.

The conclusion of the interview

• This is usually indicated when the interviewer stands up.

• Shake hands and thank him/her for considering you.

• During the interview cr shortly after, write down the name(s) of the interviewer(s) so you won't forget.

Follow up

• Thank your interviewer for their time before leaving.

• Send a thank you note via email or hand deliver within two days.

The goal of an interview is to leave a positive impression. Remind the interviewer of your interest, but avoid being annoying.

CHAPTER 2   HOW I GOT STARTED

When I was first starting out as a developer, I remember how excited I was at the mere thought of having any company interested in me. As time went on, and I moved from one company to the next, my salary grew almost exponentially and in a very short period of time. I would love to tell you that this happened because I'm a genius or that I had found the secret to the Jedi mind trick and was able to make people do what I wanted, but that would be "slightly" misleading.

The first developer job I ever had, my salary was $32,000 per year and I was extremely excited! If you do the math, you will find that dividing an annual salary by two gives you an approximate hourly rate of $16 per hour. $16 per hour to do what I love to do was amazing in my mind. Six months went by and even though I loved my job, I happened to see a job posting for another position at a startup company and decided to apply for it. It was a simple HTML developer position. They didn't even require me to be an expert. If I remember correctly, the job description said that I should have "some" knowledge of HTML. Keep in mind it was at a time when HTML was less trivial to know than it is today because standards were still being developed and the language itself was mildly esoteric.

Needless to say, I did the interview and amazingly enough, I got the job. I didn't find out until afterwards that the job paid $64,000 per year! That my friend is a two-fold increase in my salary in the first six months of being a developer! I was ecstatic! You have to believe me when I tell you that this is not an anomaly. You will see later in the book that I am a huge believer in the phrase "Fortis Fortuna Adiuvat".

The new company was amazing. Every benefit you could possibly imagine came with the job. From free gym memberships, to free food and soda all day long. There seemed to be no end. Who doesn't love and I mean LOVE free food and soda! We had lunch and dinner catered from nice restaurants and even kegs of beer brought in every Friday. This was the life and I was as happy as could be.

Fast-forward six months. My friend Bill sends me an email with a job description that a local company is hiring for. It's a six-month contract position with the possibility of extension. The pay is $50 per hour on w2 plus benefits. The job description stated that they wanted someone who had at least a few years of experience with Visual Basic and Desktop Applications development. I had neither. However, I had **some** knowledge of Visual Basic and was teaching myself the language from a book called "Learn Visual Basic in 21 Days" that I bought for $15 online.

I decided to interview just for the heck of it. Nothing ventured, nothing gained and fortune favors the bold kind of thing. In the interview, I know they're asking me fairly simple technical questions, none of which I answered correctly and all of which were over my head. I left the interview with my spirit broken and headed directly for 31 flavors to drown my sorrows in ice cream. I'm not really sure what the genetically encoded survival mechanism is that dictates "When I lose the game, it's time to get fat" but I assure you it is a strong one.

The next day, I'm back at my job, just as happy as could be and grateful for even having the job at all, as I sit stuffing myself with Snickers bars and soda. I check my email and see one from the company I just interviewed with that reads:

"Greg, thanks for coming in. We have decided that you are a good fit for this position and would like to know when you could start? The sooner the better. - David"

My first reaction was that the email was a joke on me. No one could have interviewed any worse than I did, nor have any less technical acuity per the job description. It wasn't until much later in life that I understood that most jobs look for a good personality fit over technical expertise and that as long as you seemed confident and competent, you already won 90% of the battle.

Understand that I'm very money driven at this time, so now I start calculating what $50 per hour is, as compared to my current $64,000 per year salary. If we approximate, it turns out $50 per hour is roughly $100,000 per year! My jaw drops and frankly I must have blacked out, because I don't even remember sending the email back stating how pleased I was that they wanted me and that I could start in two weeks. I packed up everything at my desk, sent my letter of resignation and never looked back.

As a side note, that startup company, which had received millions of dollars of venture capital to the tune of about 30 million dollars, having no business plan or any way to make money, went "under" two weeks after I left. I remember talking to my boss a week before I left and telling him that I couldn't believe the company is seemingly doing so well when their only product generates no income whatsoever. I say seemingly because what company would be giving away so many benefits and perks to their employees unless they were doing really well? I wasn't any kind of business expert, but I figured it common sense that at some point one would need a product or service with which to make money. Well, it turns out, management wasn't so bright and less than bright people would give away benefits and perks when they weren't making any money whatsoever. I used to think that people in E-level positions had some hidden genius, but in reality, they're really no smarter than anyone else. This entire experience was definitely a lesson learned to say the least.

So let's look at the timeline here. My first year as a developer I start out making $32,000 per year and am as excited as can be. Six months goes by and I have already doubled my income to $64,000 per year. Six more months goes by and my salary has gone up 56.25% to $100,000 per year.

Think it ends there? Think again. Just four short months go by and I decide that it's time to start my own consulting business and to go find my own clients. I am a diligent researcher at heart. If I don't know something, I am very driven to learn. I will find as much literature as I can on how something is done. I will find any person I can to help me understand the ins and outs of any process. I do as much research as possible on how to start a company and even what kind of company i.e. LLC, S-Corp, C-Corp. After all was said and done, I started an LLC because it was fast, simple and cost virtually nothing to start or maintain.

Tip: Check your states corporation commission website for information on starting your own company, if you're so inclined. It is remarkably fast and painless to start an L.L.C. (Limited Liability Company) You may or may not want to do this if you do any contract work. There are tremendous tax advantages to starting your own business and writing off all of your business expenses.

I attained my first client through word of mouth. My per hour rate? $250 per hour working 40 hour weeks and being my own boss. A 500% increase in salary. I was raking it in, kicking ass and taking names.

Keep in mind, the economy at the time was ripe for this kind of rate and businesses seemed to have no end to their cash reserves. The hype to get their business online drove the need to hire good developers, who could get the job done and companies were willing to pay top dollar in order to get it done.

Luckily, I have always had one true asset about my personality that made all of this possible. The ability to read manuals, no matter how large they were, in one sitting. I absolutely despise reading books for leisure, I always have. There is just something about reading a book for fun that irks me and I could never truly pinpoint what that was, other than to say, I hate wasting my time for something just to get "fun" as my reward. I always need to be learning something new, or honing my skills, increasing my technical acuity and striving to be the better version of myself. Manuals were a way to learn something new, brush up on skills, have more knowledge, and for me, that was the best reward I could receive for my time. 500-page manual on Python? No problem, I'll be done by the end of the day and amazingly enough will retain enough of it to be functional. Sure I didn't memorize the whole thing, but I could learn enough to get the gist and actually start getting work done. By the end of the first week I was coding with the best of them. This is how it's always been for me. If I don't know something, I'll go out and learn it as quickly as possible. I'll try and master it and be the best I can be at it.

Between the age of 25 and 30 my net worth went from negative $22,000, racked up on my credit cards, to a $500,000+ net worth, with thoughts of retiring by the age of 32. I really thought that I just needed 2 million dollars to my name and no debt to retire. I found out later that 2 million dollars might not be enough to retire on. Also, when I say retire, I truly only define it as not having to "worry" about money. I don't think I could ever stop working. It just isn't me.

CHAPTER 3   THE ART OF SALARY NEGOTIATION

This section is incredibly important. It will make the difference between an income of $60,000 per year versus $100,000 per year just by changing your mindset. Your self-confidence, self-worth and perceived confidence will sell the best version of you for the most money every time. Employers hardly ever make their best offer first, and candidates who negotiate their salary almost always earns more than those who don't. I will use rate and salary interchangeably but know that when I talk about rate, I am talking about contract work versus salary which is compensation for full-time employment.

Tip: People who at least attempt to ask for a higher salary are perceived more positively, since they're demonstrating the skills the company wants to hire them for.

Let me stop here and make a quick point. I personally guarantee that if you follow the information in these firs⁻ few chapters you will get more money for the same job hands down. On a brilliance scale from 1 to 10, I already know you're a 10 because you took the time to buy this book in order to make an additional $1k - $50k just by doing some research. I urge you to help me out, if, I have helped you out. Give me and my book rave reviews to your friends, colleagues and especially on websites like amazon.com and walmart.com. Now back to the fun.

Here's a step-by-step guide to negotiating your best salary yet:

Do your research

Before you go for an interview, you should find out what the market rates are for the job you're looking for. There are salary surveys available online, and if you're dealing with a recruitment agency, your recruiter should be able to advise you on the salary range for the position.

I'm going to repeat the following point a few times in this book to make my point. I strongly urge you to reply to every single recruiter who contacts you for the exact same position to find out what they will offer you as compensation for the position. You may be extremely surprised at the drastic range in compensation you are quoted!

Check online job boards and see what companies are offering for a particular city and area of expertise. I find that general reports on income by profession are grossly inaccurate and misleading. You need to see first-hand what companies are willing to pay. Chances are, the companies that do not post a salary or hourly rate are hiding the fact that they pay way too little. If there is no rate or salary, send them an email and apply whether you're interested or not and ask them what the rate or salary is just so you have a point of reference. The more information you have, the better you'll be able to sell yourself.

Think about what you want from the job, both in terms of the job itself and in terms of remuneration. This will help you appear more self-assured during the interview and salary negotiation process. The more specific your demands are, the better you're perceived and received by the employer.

The newest studies in business psychology show that you're perceived in an entirely different light when you come into an interview with an agenda and knowing exactly what you want out of the job. It demonstrates decisiveness, vision and forethought.

Talk money early

Tip: You should always ask about compensation before any interview. This is usually done in the pre-screen process before the real interview ever takes place. Don't waste your time and the company's time by not doing your due-diligence upfront.

While we all want to ecrn more when we change jobs, no employer wants to hire someone whose only motivation to change jobs is a higher salary. At the same time, your time is valuable and going into an interview for 4 hours only to find out it pays way less than you would even remotely find acceptable is a waste of your time and the company's time. Make sure you know exactly what the pay or pay range is up front. No matter what a recruiter or a company says, the company has a budget restriction that correlates to a range the hiring manager can work from. You need to know what this range is in order to get the best rate or salary you can.

So, how do you answer the inevitable interview question, "What salary are you looking for?" This is where your homework becomes invaluable.

Hopefully, you'll know the market rates for the type of position you're looking for. It's better to give a range rather than a specific number — you don't want to give a salary that's perhaps lower than the employer is looking to pay, but you don't want to price yourself out of the market, either. Emphasize that you're primarily interested in finding the right job for you, and that salary isn't your main consideration. But, at the same time, my immediate response is always:

"What is the very best rate (or salary) for this position?"

Believe me, you may have to ask a few times before you get an answer, but eventually you will get the information you want. The only reason why recruiters don't want to give you this information is because they want to make as much money as possible when placing you. If you don't mind giving away your money, then by all means, don't bother to ask questions. You and I both know, you want as much money as possible for your hard work and time.

Tip: Some recruiters will base what you should receive for the new position off of what you have recently made. This is unfair and frankly is wrong in my opinion. I either tell them that the information is not something I can talk about or I make up a number that matches what I expect from the new position. You are doing yourself a disservice by divulging information that will most likely be used against you.

Some recruiters have WAY more latitude than they let on.

The typical recruiter almost always has the ability to make the final decision on your compensation package. After you negotiate with them, they will need to go back and confirm the package with a hiring manager or supervisor.

In other words, the recruiter is going to sell you to the hiring manager. It's up to them to communicate why you deserve a higher salary. You want their support, because they're going to sell you at a rate that is commensurate with their impression of your personality and skill set. You can help the recruiter out by giving them justification for the compensation you're asking for and by not coming across as greedy or egotistical. The single biggest mistake that most candidates make when it comes to salary negotiation is telling the recruiter what they would be willing to accept. Most candidates don't like being pressured, so they simply blurt out a number they are willing to take — but you should never be the first one to give a number. One way to avoid this common mistake is to ask about the salary range the very first time you talk to a recruiter or hiring manager. If it's not enough, then be nice and give clear reasons for the compensation you do require. You're not battling against them; you're working with them. You would be amazed at what a little time spent negotiating can accomplish. You really have nothing to lose.

I have worked with some honest recruiters in the past and I have worked with some less than reputable ones and take my word, you need to run when you smell a rat. I remember taking a position for a company well under my normal rate just because I needed work fast and the job description made it sound easy with very little responsibility. I went back and forth with the recruiter trying to squeeze as much out of the rate as possible before finally accepting. I ended up with a rate that was $65 per hour and believe me it was a fight to the end to get this much. The recruiter also let me know that I would receive a sign on bonus if I stayed at least 30 days. This seemed sort of odd since I didn't even ask for it but I was more than willing to accept it under the circumstances.

By the third day on the job, my boss let it slip that the company was paying my recruiter $135 per hour! Let's do the math here. The recruiter is paying me $65 per hour and the company using the recruiter is paying the recruiter $135 per hour. The recruiter is making $70 per hour profit for every single hour I work. The recruiter is not only scamming me out of money but also scamming the company out of a much more experienced developer who would readily accept $100+ per hour versus $65 per hour. The company just got lucky that they hired me for that lesser rate. I guess that sign-on bonus wasn't so odd after all.

Needless to say, I re-negotiated the terms with the recruiter and was making over $100 per hour which was still far less than what the company was paying the recruiter! However, I was happier in the end, produced better work and stayed longer because of the additional money. This is a rare thing to have happen to anyone. I got lucky and although I don't recommend doing this, I will say that I would do it every single time, at the risk of losing the job. Sometimes you have to do things on principle, if you have the latitude to get away with it.

It's important to research the company and the position a recruiter is hiring for to try and get some semblance of what the position is actually paying. You will most likely receive emails from multiple recruiters for the exact same position and I urge you to respond to all of them with the following statement:

"What's the very best rate (salary) for this position?"

I think you'll be extremely surprised at the responses you get. The exact same position for the exact same company will have a dramatically different range of compensation depending on who the recruiter is.

Example: I received 10 emails from different recruiters for a senior architect position with a company (Let's call the company XYZ) and to each recruiter, I responded asking what the very best rate for the position was. I was floored by the responses I received which were anywhere from $50 per hour to $125 per hour for the exact same position with the exact same job requisition number!

Shop around and find the best recruiter you can. It makes a dramatic difference. After all, a recruiter represents you and is tied to you for the duration of the contract. If it's a full time position, that's a different story but I leave it up to you to make the right choice as to whether you feel comfortable with the recruiter you're dealing with.

Believe that you CAN negotiate in this economy

Henry Ford said "Whether you think you can, or you think you can't--you're right." Your belief about your self-worth and your level of self-confidence can take you further than any other skill you have. You must believe you deserve the most money you can get from a position. Pretend you're your own talent manager and write down your strengths as if you were going to sell yourself. If you don't believe you deserve every penny you're worth, why should anyone else? You might as well stop reading now, because no amount of information is ever going to help you get ahead if you lack the self-confidence to walk the walk. If you believe it, you can achieve it.

Don't be afraid to ask — But don't demand, either

Know what your worth is and don't be afraid to ask for it. No one loses a job offer because they ask questions — however, you can have a job offer pulled because of the way you ask them. It's important that your salary or rate request is within the ballpark of the range for the position, so avoid giving a specific number until the employer is ready to make you an offer. Remember to be enthusiastic, polite and professional during negotiations. Communicate to your prospective employer through your tone of voice and demeanor, that your goal is a win-win solution. If you're too pushy, the employer may get the impression that you're not that interested in the job (or only interested in the money) and withdraw the offer.

Keep selling yourself

As you go through the interviewing and negotiating process, remind the employer how they'll benefit from your skills and experience. Let's say, for example, that the employer wants to offer $70K, but you're looking for minimum $90K base salary. Explain how they'd benefit by increasing your compensation.

For example:

> *"I realize you have a budget to worry about. However, I believe that with the desktop publishing and graphic design skills I bring to the position, you won't have to hire outside vendors to produce customer newsletters and other publications. That alone should produce far more than $20K in savings a year."*

In other words, justify every additional dollar or benefit you request. Remember to do so by focusing on the employer's needs, not yours.

Make them jealous

If you're interviewing for other jobs, you might want to tell employers about those offers. This should speed up the acceptance process. If they know you have another offer, you'll seem more attractive to them, and it might help you negotiate a higher salary.

Tip: Sometimes when asked, I conjure other offers and interviews out of thin air. I do this to invoke a need of immediacy in order to get everyone moving as quickly as possible and to give myself some additional leverage when requesting compensation for a position. Get good at the bluff, it will serve you well.

Ask for a fair price

Again, you really need to ensure your compensation requests are reasonable and in line with the current marketplace. If the salary offer is below market value, you might want to gently suggest it's in the company's best interest to pay the going rate:

"The research that I've done indicates the going rate for a position such as this is $6K higher than this offer. I'd really love to work for you and I believe I can add a lot of value in this job; however, I can't justify doing so for less than market value. I think if you reevaluate the position and consider its importance to your bottom line, you'll find it's worth paying market price to get someone who can really make an impact quickly."

Negotiate extras and be creative!

If the employer can't offer you the salary you want, think about other valuable options that might not cost them as much. You can look at negotiating holiday days (e.g. if new employees must work for 6 to 12 months before receiving paid holidays, ask that this restriction be waived.), ask for yearly salary reviews or negotiate a sign-on or performance bonus.

Be confident

Remember to use confident body language and speech patterns. When you make a salary request, don't go on and on, stating over and over why it's justified. Make your request and offer a short, simple explanation of why that amount is appropriate.

Tip: It's a smart negotiating strategy to ask for a few benefits or perks you don't want that badly. Then you can "give in" and agree to take the job without those added benefits, if, the employer meets all of your other requests.

Ideally, both parties in a negotiation should come away from the table feeling that they've won. This is especially true when you're dealing with salary negotiations. You want employers to have good feelings about the price paid for your services so that your working relationship begins on a positive note.

Keep track of what you have done well

The greatest tool that you have in any interview is proof. Keep examples of your best work, thank you notes from clients, awards or recognitions, and positive work evaluations. Once you discover what is important to the company and how your skills can meet those needs, you can then use these items as proof of the value you can provide. It's a lot easier to get a higher salary when you have proof of why you deserve it.

Don't take it personally

Easier said than done? Not with practice. Maybe you'll get what you want. Maybe you won't. Life will move on either way. Most people will never have a negotiation that will make or break their life. Keep it real and don't get emotionally involved. If you ask for more than the job is willing to pay, let them call your bluff. It's going to be a numbers game and the more you play the game, the better you'll be at it and the more money you will make for the exact same 40 hours a week. Get the most money for your time!

CHAPTER 4   HOW TO BECOME A REMOTE WORKER

There are three ways to become a telecommuter or remote worker. The first, is if the job requirement states it's a telecommuting position. The second, is to convince your boss that should telecommute and the third, is to be your own boss, so you make the rules and deal only with clients who will allow telecommuting.

As a design project manager at a top Internet marketing firm, my dear friend Mary loved her job but couldn't stand the commute. When the price of gas soared to over $4 a gallon, she realized she was spending a small fortune getting to and from her office in downtown Los Angeles.

Mary had been with the company for four years and was already working at home one day a week. Now she chanced negotiating a permanent telecommuting arrangement with her boss.

"Because our company has a core value promoting a healthy work-life balance, all of our major software is available remotely. Because we have Internet phone lines, I thought my boss might be amenable to it," she says. "When I approached my boss, I mentioned my existing productivity working from home and how I felt that we could continue to measure that success while telecommuting full-time. I promised to be available to my clients during normal business hours and to return to the office two days a month for meetings or whenever there was an emergency."

Mary spent about 20 minutes coming up with and documenting this letter. That 20 minutes reaped enormous benefits that she would not have enjoyed otherwise, if it weren't for a little self-confidence and the belief that it was possible.

Mary has never been happier. "I get to work from home and also know I have a secure, reliable job." Her arrangement isn't unique. Organizations around the world are implementing telework with enthusiasm. According to a 2014 study by the American Electronics Association, 47 million Americans already telecommute at least one day a week.

BT, a leading provider of communications solutions, hired its first home worker in 1986; today more than 70% of BT's employees benefit from flexible working.

The company estimates that it has saved at least $500 million and has improved its productivity by between 15% and 31%.

How do you determine if telecommuting is for you? Michael Randall, a productivity expert, says the best candidates are people who are disciplined and self-motivated: "When your boss says, 'Here's a project, figure it out by this deadline,' do you get it done? Can you stay focused despite distractions and see a task through to completion?" He also says you need to be naturally organized and skilled at time management:

> *"People who work from home should be able to schedule realistically and prioritize correctly."*

If you think you fit the bill, your first step in making telecommuting a reality is to talk with someone in human resources to find out just how your organization's flexible work policy works. Don't despair if there's no official policy in place. There may be others in your department telecommuting successfully, and if you establish a high level of trust with your manager, broaching the issue won't be unreasonable.

To make the argument for telecommuting, prepare a written proposal that puts the organization first and addresses, upfront, the issues you know your boss will be concerned about. The key is to present teleworking as a benefit to the employer.

I was once offered a contracting position in which I explained that I could get the same amount of work done in three-quarters of the time from my own office–without the usual interruptions that comes with working in a room full of people. It would also be one fewer desk, phone and computer the company had to provide and one more notch in their belt as an earth-friendly employer that does what it can to keep cars off the road.

Your proposal should detail how you'll set up your home office, and it should assure your manager that you will have a clean, quiet and child-free work environment in which to complete your duties. Your boss will want to know that you have a fast Internet connection, a dedicated phone number and all the necessary supplies.

Suggest a trial period for the telecommuting arrangement after which you and your manager can evaluate how it's working. Once you're off and running, make a conscious effort to show your boss that you're cutting expenses and getting more work done faster. Make sure you're always accessible via e-mail and cellphone during the business day, and report often on where projects stand, so your boss can easily keep tabs on you.

Telecommuting shouldn't mean you never see the inside of the office building again. If you supervise other employees, or make presentations about your initiatives, or are a key participant in team meetings, show up in person as often as you can. Telecommuting must not compromise the critical workplace relationships you've spent time and energy building.

If you're currently job hunting and want to get into a telework situation right from the start, you can turn to a variety of websites that list such positions. FlexJobs.com, for example, is a low-cost subscription service that identifies and screens legitimate telecommuting jobs. Just be aware that telework positions tend to be much more competitive, so your resume should detail a history of independent work that produced stellar results.

When searching job boards online, you will want to use keywords like "Remote, virtual or telecommute" in order to find these kind of jobs. Important to note is that I find more often than not, the word "remote" is in many job descriptions that aren't telecommuting jobs at all, but deal with remote (outsourced) teams.

Also keep in mind that most remote positions pay less and are usually salary based, as opposed to hourly, but that doesn't mean you can't inquire about the position and ask if it can be done on a contractual basis. Be sure to send your references and a job history that includes all of the remote work you've done.

CHAPTER 5 CLOUD TERMINOLOGY

1. Airframe

An open source cloud computing platform targeted at organizations in the thinking stage of adopting a private cloud services model or evaluating options and alternatives for private cloud solutions.

2. Amazon EC2

Short for Amazon Elastic Computer Cloud, Amazon EC2 is a commercial Web service that lets customers "rent" computing resources from the EC2 cloud.

3. Anything-as-a-Service

Anything-as-a-service, or XaaS, refers to the growing diversity of services available over the Internet via cloud computing as opposed to being provided locally, or on premises.

4. Apache CloudStack

An open source cloud computing and Infrastructure-as-a-Service (IaaS) platform developed to help make creating, deploying and managing cloud services easier by providing a complete "stack" of features and components for cloud environments.

5. Business analytics tools

Tools that extract data from business systems and integrate it into a repository, such as a data warehouse, where it can be analyzed. Analytics tools range from spreadsheets with statistical functions to sophisticated data mining and predictive modeling tools.

6. Business intelligence (BI) tools

Tools that process large amounts of unstructured data in books, journals, documents, health records, images, files, email, video, and so forth, to help you discover meaningful trends and identify new business opportunities.

7. Cloud

A metaphor for a global network, first used in reference to the telephone network and now commonly used to represent the Internet.

8. Cloud App (Cloud Application)

Short for cloud application, cloud app is the phrase used to describe a software application that is never installed on a local computer. Instead, it is accessed via the Internet.

9. Cloud Application Management for Platforms (CAMP)

CAMP, short for Cloud Application Management for Platforms, is a specification designed to ease management of applications -- including packaging and deployment -- across public and private cloud computing platforms.

10. Cloud Backup

Cloud backup, or cloud computer backup, refers to backing up data to a remote, cloud-based server. As a form of cloud storage, cloud backup data is stored in and accessible from multiple distributed and connected resources that comprise a cloud.

11. Cloud Backup Service Provider

A third-party entity that manages and distributes remote, cloud-based data backup services and solutions to customers from a central data center.

12. Cloud Backup Solutions

Cloud backup solutions enable enterprises or individuals to store their data and computer files on the Internet using a storage service provider, rather than storing the data locally on a physical disk, such as a hard drive or tape backup.

13. Cloud bursting

A configuration that's set up between a private cloud and a public cloud. If 100 percent of the resource capacity is used in a private cloud, then overflow traffic is directed to the public cloud using cloud bursting.

14. Cloud Computing

A type of computing, comparable to grid computing that relies on sharing computing resources rather than having local servers or personal devices to handle applications. The goal of cloud computing is to apply traditional supercomputing, or high-performance computing power, normally used by military and research facilities, to perform tens of trillions of computations per second, in consumer-oriented applications such as financial portfolios or even to deliver personalized information, or power immersive computer games.

15. *Cloud Computing Accounting Software*

Cloud computing accounting software is accounting software that is hosted on remote servers. It provides accounting capabilities to businesses in a fashion similar to the SaaS (Software as a Service) business model. Data is sent into "the cloud," where it is processed and returned to the user. All application functions are performed off-site, not on the user's desktop.

16. *Cloud Computing Reseller*

A company that purchases hosting services from a cloud server hosting or cloud computing provider and then re-sells them to its own customers.

17. *Cloud computing types*

There are three main cloud computing types, with additional ones evolving: software-as-a-service (SaaS) for web-based applications, infrastructure-as-a-service (IaaS) for Internet-based access to storage and computing power, and platform-as-a-service (PaaS) that gives developers the tools to build and host Web applications.

18. Cloud Database

A database accessible to clients from the cloud and delivered to users on demand via the Internet from a cloud database provider's servers. Also referred to as Database-as-a-Service (DBaaS), cloud databases can use cloud computing to achieve optimized scaling, high availability, multi-tenancy and effective resource allocation.

19. Cloud Enablement

The process of making available one or more of the following services and infrastructures to create a public cloud computing environment: cloud provider, client and application.

20. Cloud Management

Software and technologies designed for operating and monitoring the applications, data and services residing in the cloud. Cloud management tools help ensure a company's cloud computing-based resources are working optimally and properly interacting with users and other services.

21. Cloud Migration

The process of transitioning all or part of a company's data, applications and services from on-site premises behind the firewall to the cloud, where the information can be provided over the Internet on an on-demand basis.

22. Cloud OS

A phrase frequently used in place of Platform as a Service (PaaS) to denote an association to cloud computing.

23. Cloud Portability

In cloud (cloud computing) terminology, the phrase "cloud portability" means the ability to move applications and its associated data between one cloud provider and another -- or between public and private cloud environments.

24. Cloud Provider

A service provider who offers customers storage or software solutions available via a public network, usually the Internet.

25. Cloud Provisioning

The deployment of a company's cloud computing strategy, which typically first involves selecting which applications and services will reside in the public cloud and which will remain on site behind the firewall or in the private cloud. Cloud provisioning also entails developing the processes for interfacing with the cloud's applications and services as well as auditing and monitoring who accesses and utilizes the resources.

26. Cloud Server Hosting

Cloud server hosting is a type of hosting in which hosting services are made available to customers on demand via the Internet. Rather than being provided by a single server or virtual server, cloud server hosting services are provided by multiple connected servers that comprise a cloud.

27. Cloud Storage

Cloud storage means "the storage of data online in the cloud," wherein a company's data is stored in and accessible from multiple distributed and connected resources that comprise a cloud.

28. Cloud Testing

Load and performance testing conducted on the applications and services provided via cloud computing -- particularly the capability to access these services -- in order to ensure optimal performance and scalability under a wide variety of conditions.

29. Computer grids

Groups of networked computers that act together to perform large tasks, such as analyzing huge sets of data and weather modeling. Cloud computing lets you assemble and use vast computer grids for specific time periods and purposes, paying only for your usage, and saving the time and expense of purchasing and deploying the necessary resources yourself.

30. Desktop-as-a-service

Desktop-as-a-service (DaaS) is a form of virtual desktop infrastructure (VDI) in which the VDI is outsourced and handled by a third party. Also called hosted desktop services, desktop-as-a-service is frequently delivered as a cloud service along with the apps needed for use on the virtual desktop.

31. *Elastic computing*

The ability to dynamically provision and de-provision computer processing, memory, and storage resources to meet changing demands without worrying about capacity planning and engineering for peak usage.

32. *Enterprise Application*

The term used to describe applications -- or software -- that a business would use to assist the organization in solving enterprise problems. When the word "enterprise" is combined with "application," it usually refers to a software platform that is too large and too complex for individual or small business use.

33. *Enterprise Cloud Backup*

Enterprise-grade cloud backup solutions typically add essential features such as archiving and disaster recovery to cloud backup solutions.

34. *Eucalyptus*

An open source cloud computing and Infrastructure-as-a-Service (IaaS) platform for enabling private clouds.

35. *Hybrid Cloud Storage*

A combination of public cloud storage and private cloud storage where some critical data resides in the enterprise's private cloud while other data is stored and accessible from a public cloud storage provider.

36. *IBM Cloud*

IBM Cloud refers to a collection of enterprise-class technologies and services developed to help customers assess their cloud readiness, develop adoption strategies and identify business entry points for a cloud environment. IBM's cloud computing strategy is based on a hybrid cloud model that focuses on integrating the private cloud services of a company with the public cloud.

37. IBM CloudBurst (CloudBurst)

CloudBurst is a "ready-to-go" solution from IBM that's designed to provide resource monitoring, cost management and services availability in a cloud. IBM CloudBurst is a key component in the company's lineup of cloud computing solutions, which also includes IBM Smart Business Storage Cloud, IBM Smart Desktop Cloud and IBMSmartCloud Enterprise.

38. Infrastructure-as-a-Service

IaaS is defined as computer infrastructure, such as virtualization, being delivered as a service. IaaS is popular in the data center where software and servers are purchased as a fully outsourced service and usually billed on usage and how much of the resource is used - compared to the traditional method of buying software and servers outright. May also be called enterprise-level hosting platform.

39. Internal Cloud

Another name for a private cloud.

40. Microsoft Azure

The Microsoft cloud platform, a growing collection of integrated services, including infrastructure as a service (IaaS) and platform as a service (PaaS) offerings. Learn more about Azure.

41. *Middleware*

Software that lies between an operating system and the applications running on it. It enables communication and data management for distributed applications, like cloud-based applications, so, for example, the data in one database can be accessed through another database. Examples of middleware are web servers, application servers, and content management systems.

42. *Mobile Cloud Storage*

A form of cloud storage that applies to storing an individual's mobile device data in the cloud and providing the individual with access to the data from anywhere.

43. *Multi-Tenant*

In cloud computing, multi-tenant is the phrase used to describe multiple customers using the same public cloud.

44. Online Backup

In storage technology, online backup means to back up data from your hard drive to a remote server or computer using a network connection. Online backup technology leverages the Internet and cloud computing to create an attractive off-site storage solution with little hardware requirements for any business of any size.

45. OpenStack Grizzly

The follow-up to the Folsom release of the OpenStack open source cloud computing platform, OpenStack Grizzly debuted in April 2013 as the seventh release of OpenStack. With OpenStack Grizzly, the OpenStack Foundation has focused on adding broader support for compute, storage and networking technologies as well as greater scalability and ease of operations.

46. Personal Cloud Storage

A form of cloud storage that applies to storing an individual's data in the cloud and providing the individual with access to the data from anywhere. Personal cloud storage also often enables syncing and sharing stored data across multiple devices such as mobile phones and tablet computers.

47. *Platform as a service (PaaS)*

A computing platform (operating system and other services) delivered as a service over the Internet by a provider. An example is an application development environment that you can subscribe to and use immediately. Azure offers PaaS. Discover the advantages of PacS.

48. *Private Cloud*

The phrase used to describe a cloud computing platform that is implemented within the corporate firewall, under the control of the IT department. A private cloud is designed to offer the same features and benefits of cloud systems, but removes a number of objections to the cloud computing model including control over enterprise and customer data, worries about security, and issues connected to regulatcry compliance.

49. Private Cloud Project

Companies initiate private cloud projects to enable their IT infrastructure to become more capable of quickly adapting to continually evolving business needs and requirements. Private cloud projects can also be connected to public clouds to create hybrid clouds.

50. Private Cloud Security

A private cloud implementation aims to avoid many of the objections regarding cloud computing security. Because a private cloud setup is implemented safely within the corporate firewall, it remains under the control of the IT department.

51. Private Cloud Storage

A form of cloud storage where the enterprise data and cloud storage resources both reside within the enterprise's data center and behind the firewall.

52. Public Cloud Storage

A form of cloud storage where the enterprise and storage service provider are separate and the data is stored outside of the enterprise's data center.

53. *Red Hat Cloud Computing*

Red Hat Cloud Computing refers to solutions for private clouds, hybrid clouds, and public clouds offered by Red Hat.

54. *Red Hat CloudForms*

Red Hat CloudForms is an Infrastructure-as-a-Service (IaaS) offering that builds upon a collection of more than 60 open source projects. CloudForms include application lifecycle management capabilities as well as the capability to create hybrid public and private clouds from the broadest range of computing resources with unique portability across physical, virtual and cloud computing resources.

55. *Red Hat OpenShift*

OpenShift provides developers with a choice in languages, frameworks, and clouds to build, test, run, and manage Java, Ruby, PHP, Perl and Python applications. Developers can also choose the cloud provider the applications will run on.

56. *Software as a Service*

SaaS is a software delivery method that provides access to software and its functions remotely as a

Web-based service. Software as a Service allows organizations to access business functionality at a cost typically less than paying for licensed applications since SaaS pricing is based on a monthly fee.

57. *Software Plus Services*

Software Plus Services (Software + Services) is Microsoft's philosophy for complementing the software company's on-premises software offerings with cloud-based remote computing software options.

58. *Storage Cloud*

Storage cloud refers to the collection of multiple distributed and connected resources responsible for storing and managing data online in the cloud.

59. *Vertical Cloud Computing*

A vertical cloud, or vertical cloud computing, is the phrase used to describe the optimization of cloud computing and cloud services for a particular vertical (e.g., a specific industry) or specific use application.

60. *Virtual machine*

A computer file (typically called an image) that behaves like an actual computer. Multiple virtual machines can run simultaneously on the same physical computer. Lecrn more about Azure Virtual Machines.

61. *Virtualization*

The act of creating a virtual rather than a physical version of a computing environment, including computer hardware, operating system, storage devices, and so forth.

62. *VMware vCloud Connector*

The VMware vCloud Connector is a tool that facilitates hybrid cloud computing for organizations. The vCloud Connector essentially helps to orchestrate and admirister the migration of VMs across different data centers and clouds.

CHAPTER 6   CLOUD INTERVIEW QUESTIONS

1. What is cloud computing?

Cloud computing is defined as the practice of using a network of remote servers hosted on the Internet to store, manage, and process data, rather than a local server or a personal computer.

2. What are the advantages of using cloud computing?

Some advantages of cloud computing are:

- Scalable and dynamic, resources can be added quickly on-demand.
- Reduced IT resource requirement
- Self-service reduces lead time and administrative overhead.
- Simplified data backup and storage
- Utilize hardware without purchasing it.
- Rapid prototyping and proof of concept capabilities.
- Exponential increase in productivity

- Cost effective & time saving

3. What are some of the major cloud providers?

1. AWS – Amazon Web Services EC2
2. DigitalOcean
3. Linode
4. Vexxhost
5. Google Computing Engine
6. Rackspace
7. Packet
8. Salesforce
9. Microsoft Azure
10. VMware vCloud Air
11. OpenStack Compute

4. Provide examples of platforms used for large scale cloud computing?

There are a multitude of platforms available for cloud computing, but to model large scale distributed computing, two major platforms are:

1. **MapReduce:** is software that is being built by Google to support distributed computing. It is a framework that works on large set of data. It utilizes the cloud resources and distributes the data to several other computers known as

clusters. It has the capability to deal with both structured and non-structured data.
2. **Apache Hadoop:** is an open source distributed computing platform. It is being written in Java. It creates a pool of computer each with Hadoop file system. It then clusters the data elements and applies the hash algorithms that are similar. Then it creates copy of the files that already exist.

5. What are the different cloud deployment models?

The different deployment models in cloud computing are:

1. Private Cloud
2. Public Cloud
3. Community Cloud
4. Hybrid Cloud

6. What are the different computing models?

There are four main computing models:

1. SaaS (Software as a service)
2. PaaS (Platform as a service)
3. IaaS (Infrastructure as a service)
4. SECaaS (Security as a service)

Cloud Deployment Models –
Advantages and Characteristics

Public Cloud
- Shifts CapEx to OpEx
- Offers a *Pay as you go* (Utility Billing) Model
- Supports Multiple Tenants

Hybrid Cloud
- Bridges one or more Private, Public or Community clouds
- Allows manipulation of CapEx and OpEx to reduce costs
- Supports Resource Portability

Community Cloud
- Allows sharing of CapEx and OpEx to reduce costs
- Brings together groups or organizations with a common goal/interest
- Supports Resource Portability

Private Cloud
- Leverages existing CapEx
- Can help reduce OpEx
- Intended for a Single Tenant

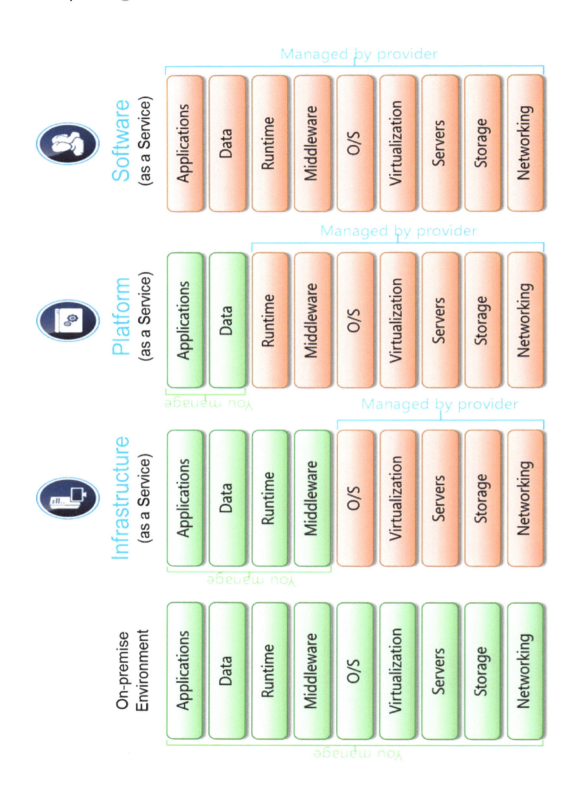

7. What are some features of SaaS?

- Service provider looks after the application
- Customer requires limited IT knowledge
- Minimal software deployed on client computers
- Often accessed via a web browser

8. What are some features of PaaS?

- Software development knowledge required
- Service provider maintains the platform
- Customer provides data and configuration only
- Customer maintains the application only

9. What are some features of IaaS?

- IT infrastructure knowledge is required
- The cloud service provider maintains hardware
- Customer maintains servers and applications
- Customer provisions virtual machines
- Suitable for legacy applications and scenarios where PaaS is not available.

10. What are some general services provided by the cloud?

- Storage
- Virtual Networks
- Virtual Machines

- Backup and Site Recovery
- Active Directory
- Remote application management
- Web Hosting

11. What does Hybrid Cloud refer to?

Hybrid cloud is a cloud computing environment which uses a mix of on-premises, private cloud and third-party public cloud services with orchestration between the two platforms. By allowing workloads to move between private and public clouds as computing needs and costs change, hybrid cloud gives businesses greater flexibility and more data deployment options.

12. What does Community Cloud refer to?

A community cloud is a multi-tenant infrastructure that is shared among several organizations from a specific group with common computing concerns. Such concerns might be related to regulatory compliance, such as audit requirements, or may be related to performance requirements, such as hosting applications that require a quick response time.

13. *What does the term utility computing refer to?*

Utility computing, or The Computer Utility, is a service provisioning model in which a service provider makes computing resources and infrastructure management available to the customer as needed, and charges them for specific usage rather than a flat rate. Like other types of on-demand computing (such as grid computing), the utility model seeks to maximize the efficient use of resources and/or minimize associated costs. Utility is the packaging of computing resources, such as computation, storage and services, as a metered service. This model has the advantage of a low or no initial cost to acquire computer resources; instead, computationa resources are essentially rented.

14. *What are some benefits of Cloud Computing?*

1. Business continuity or disaster recovery is often the responsibility of the cloud provider.
2. The cloud allows for "as a service" model which shifts expenditure from capital to operational expenses. Organizations pay for cloud services without the need to buy hardware.

15. What security aspects are provided by cloud providers?

a. Identity management: It authorizes the application services.
b. Access control: permission has to be provided to the users so that they can control the access of another user who is entering into the cloud environment.
c. Authentication and Authorization: Allows only the authorized and authenticated user only to access the data and applications.

16. List out different layers which define cloud architecture?

The different layers used by cloud architecture are:

a. CLC or Cloud Controller
b. Walrus
c. Cluster Controller
d. SC or Storage Controller
e. NC or Node Controller

17. What are system integrators in Cloud Computing?

In Cloud Computing, systems integrator provides the strategy of the complicated process used to design a cloud platform. Integrator allows to create more accurate hybrid and private cloud network, as integrators have all the knowledge about the data center creation.

18. What does "EUCALYPTUS" stands for?

"EUCALYPTUS" stands for Elastic Utility Computing Architecture For Linking Your Programs To Useful Systems.

19. Explain what is the use of "EUCALYPTUS" in cloud computing?

"Eucalyptus" is an open source software infrastructure in cloud computing, which is used to implement clusters in cloud computing platform. It is used to build public, hybrid and private clouds. It has the ability to produce your own data center into a private cloud and allows you to use its functionality to many other organizations.

20. What is the requirement of virtualization platform in implementing cloud?

The requirement of virtualization platform in implementing cloud is to

a. Manage the service level policies
b. Cloud Operating System
c. Virtualization platforms helps to keep the backend level and user level concepts different from each other.

21. Before going for cloud computing platform what are the essential things to be taken in concern by users?

a. Compliance
b. Loss of data
c. Data storage
d. Business continuity
e. Uptime
f. Data integrity in cloud computing

22. Mention some open source cloud computing platform databases?

The open source cloud computing platform databases are:

1. MongoDB
2. CouchDB
3. LucidDB

23. What are the security laws which are implemented to secure data in a cloud?

The security laws which are implemented to secure data in cloud are:

a. Processing: Control the data that is being processed correctly and completely in an application
b. File: It manages and control the data being manipulated in any of the file
c. Output reconciliation: It controls the data which has to be reconciled from input to output
d. Input Validation: Control the input data
e. Security and Backup: It provides security and backup it also controls the security breaches logs

24. Mention the name of some large cloud providers and databases?

a. Google bigtable
b. Amazon SimpleDB
c. Cloud based SQL

25. Explain the difference between cloud and traditional datacenters?

a. The cost of the traditional data center is higher due to heating and hardware/software issues

b. Cloud gets scaled when the demand increases. Majority of the expenses are spent on the maintenance of the data centers, while that is not the case with cloud computing.

26. *Explain what are the different modes of software as a service (SaaS)?*

a. Simple multi-tenancy: In this each user has independent resources and are different from other users, it is an efficient mode.
b. Fine grain multi-tenancy: In this type, the resources can be shared by many but the functionality remains the same.

27. *What is the use of API's in cloud services?*

API's (Application Programming Interface) are very useful in cloud platforms:

a. They eliminate the need to write fully fledged programs
b. They provide allow communication between one or more applications
c. They allow abstraction, encapsulation and loose-coupling of logic for applications.

28. What are the different data centers deployed for cloud computing?

- Containerized Datacenters
- Low Density Datacenters

29. In cloud computing what are the different layers?

The different layers of cloud computing are:

1. SaaS: Software as a Service (SaaS), it provides users access directly to the cloud application without installing anything on the system.
2. IaaS: Infrastructure as a service, it provides the infrastructure in terms of hardware like memory, processor speed etc.
3. PaaS: Platform as a service, it provides cloud application platform for the developers
4. SECaaS: Security as a service, provides authentication and authorization to cloud resources.

30. How important is the platform as a service?

Platform as a service or PAAS is an important layer in cloud computing. It provides application platform for providers. It is responsible for providing complete virtualization of the infrastructure layer and makes it work like a single server.

31. What is a cloud service?

Cloud service is used to build cloud applications using the server in a network through internet. It provides the facility of using the cloud application without installing it on the computer. It also reduces the maintenance and support of the application which are developed using cloud service.

32. List down the three basic clouds in cloud computing?

a. Professional cloud
b. Personal cloud
c. Performance cloud

33. What resources are provided in infrastructure as a service (IaaS)?

IAAS (Infrastructure as a Service) provides virtual and physical resources that are used to build a cloud. It deals with the complexities of deploying and maintaining of the services provided by this layer. Here the infrastructure is the servers, storage and other hardware systems.

34. What are the business benefits involved in cloud architecture?

- Zero infrastructure investment
- Just in time infrastructure
- More efficient resource utilization

35. What are the characteristics of cloud architecture that separates it from traditional one?

- According to demand, cloud architecture provides the hardware requirement.
- Cloud architecture is capable of scaling the resource on demand.
- Cloud architecture is capable of managing and handling dynamic workloads without failure.

36. Mention what is the difference between elasticity and scalability in cloud computing?

Scalability is a characteristics of cloud computing through which increasing workload can be handled by increasing in proportion the amount of resource capacity. Whereas, elasticity, is being one of the characteristics that highlights the concept of commissioning and decommissioning of a large amount of resource capacity.

37.   What services are provided by Microsoft Azure?

1. Compute
2. Storage
3. Management
4. Security

38.   In cloud architecture what are the different components that are required?

- Cloud Ingress
- Processor Speed
- Cloud storage services
- Cloud provided services
- Intra-cloud communications

39.   In cloud architecture, what four phases are involved?

1. Launch
2. Monitor
3. Shutdown
4. Cleanup

40.   What basic characteristics comprise cloud computing?

1. Elasticity and Scalability

2. Self-service provisioning and automatic de-provisioning
3. Standardized interfaces
4. Billing self-service based usage model

41. In cloud architecture what are the building blocks?

a. Reference architecture
b. Technical architecture
c. Deployment operation architecture

42. In what ways does cloud architecture provide automation and performance transparency?

Through logging, monitoring and analytics of metrics.

43. In cloud computing, explain the role of performance cloud?

Performance cloud deals with transferring large data-sets in near real-time. It's used by professionals who work in high performance computing research.

44. In cloud what are the optimizing strategies?

To overcome the maintenance cost and to optimize the resources, there is a concept of three data center in cloud which provides recovery and back-up in case of disaster or system failure and keeps all the data safe and intact.

45. What is Amazon SQS?

To communicate between different connectors Amazon SQS message is used, between various components of AMAZON, it acts as a communicator.

46. How Buffer is used in Amazon web services?

In order to make system more efficient against the burst of traffic or load, Buffer is used. It synchronizes different components. The component always receives and processes the request in an unbalanced way. The balance between different components are managed by Buffer, and makes them work at the same speed to provide faster services.

47. Mention what is Hypervisor in cloud computing and their types?

Hypervisor is a Virtual Machine Monitor which manages resources for virtual machines. There are mainly two types of hypervisors

Type 1: The guest VM runs directly over the host hardware e.g. Xen, VMWare ESXI

Type 2: The guest VM runs over hardware through a host operating system e.g. KVM, Oracle Virtual Box

CHAPTER 7   AZURE INTERVIEW QUESTIONS

1. What are the different categories of services available in Azure?

- Compute
- Web & Mobile
- Data & Storage
- Intelligence
- Analytics
- Internet of Things
- Networking
- Media & CDN
- Hybrid Integration
- Identity & Access Management
- Developer Services
- Management

2. Does Azure support Linux-based virtual machines?

Yes

3. What is Azure DNS?

Available for use in all public Azure regions, Azure DNS lets customers hos¯ their Domain Name System (DNS) domains in Azure and manage DNS records using the same credentials, APIs, tools, billing, and support as their other Azure services. Azure DNS also incorporates enterprise-grade security features in Azure Resource Manager for two-factor authentication, role-based access control, and detailed audit logs. Azure DNS uses a global network of name servers for extremely high performance and availability, now backed by a 99.99 percent availability service-level agreement (SLA). Azure DNS pricing is based on the number of hosted DNS zones and the number of DNS queries received (in millions).

4. What is Virtual Network Peering?

Virtual network peering for Azure Virtual Network lets customers directly link virtual machines in two virtual networks in the same region through private IP addresses, as if they were part of the same network. Virtual network peering routes packets through the internal Azure backbone network—without any gateway in the path. This allows for low-latency, high-bandwidth connections between virtual machines in different virtual networks. Virtual network peering also allows transit through the peered virtual networks, so a network virtual appliance or a VPN gateway in one virtual network can be used by a virtual machine in another peered virtual network. Peering works across virtual networks in different subscriptions and between an Azure Resource Manager (V2) and Azure Classic (V1) virtual network. It does not work between two Azure Classic virtual networks. For more information, please visit the VNet peering documentation webpage.

5. What is the Application Gateway Web Application Firewall (WAF)?

The web application firewall (WAF) in Azure Application Gateway protects web applications from common web-based attacks like SQL injection, cross-site scripting attacks, and session hijacks. It comes preconfigured with protection from threats identified by the Open Web Application Security Project (OWASP) as the top 10 common vulnerabilities. The firewall is simple to deploy and provides logging to continuously monitor web applications against exploits. Customers can run

Application Gateway WAF in both protection and detection-only modes.

6. What functionality does HTTP/2 support for Azure Content Delivery Network from Akamai standard provide?

HTTP/2 improves user experience by increasing webpage loading speed and performance. This feature is now enabled by default at no additional cost for all customers using Azure Content Delivery Network from Akamai. The HTTP/2 edge server implementation is fully compliant with the HTTP/2 standard RFC 7540. (All HTTP/2 features are supported with the exception of server push.)

Main HTTP/2 features include:

1. Multiplexing, which allows multiple requests to be sent on the same TCP connection.

2. Header compression, to reduce header size in a request.

3. Stream prioritization, to transfer important data first.

7. What are the H-Series instances for Azure Virtual Machines?

H-Series instances for Azure Virtual Machines will be among the fastest virtual machines available in Azure in terms of performance per core (ACU benchmark). Depending on application and scenario offering, it gets as much as a 30 to 50 percent performance increase compared to other virtual machines.

H-Series instances are for high-end computational needs, like molecular modeling and computational fluid dynamics. They're built on Intel Haswell E5-2667 v3 processors, with 8- and 16-core virtual machine sizes featuring DDR4 memory and local solid-state drive (SSD) storage. Besides substantial CPU power, the H-Series offers diverse options for remote direct memory access (RDMA) and low-latency networking using FDR InfiniBand along with several memory configurations to support memory-intensive computational requirements.

8. Accelerated Networking for Azure Virtual Machines?

Customers now expect the performance of their virtual machines to be comparable to a physical box they can buy themselves. Accelerated Networking for Windows virtual machines on Azure offers up to 25 Gbps networking speeds. That means customers can achieve near-native performance on Windows virtual machines in the cloud, likely surpassing typical on-premises performance in terms of the speed and consistency that their applications require. Accelerated Networking is now available in public preview for select virtual machine types and regions at no extra charge.

9. What is the impact of utilizing virtual machine-based services with new IPv6 for Azure Virtual Machines?

The Internet has expanded beyond the capacity of the IPv4 protocol. Many new mobile networks and new technologies, such as the Internet of Things (IoT), depend on the nearly unlimited address capacity offered by IPv6. Now Azure-hosted services offer Azure IPv6-load-balanced, dual-stack (IPv4+IPv6) Internet connectivity for Azure Virtual Machines. Native IPv6 connectivity (TCP, UDP, HTTP(S)) all the way to the virtual machine enables a broad range of service architectures. IPv6 for Virtual Machines is available now in most Azure regions.

10. Explain Azure Disk Encryption for Windows and Linux Standard and Premium IaaS virtual machines.

Azure Disk Encryption for Linux IaaS virtual machines and support for virtual machines with Premium storage is generally available in all Azure public regions. Azure Disk Encryption for Windows and Linux Standard IaaS virtual machines is now generally available to enable customers to protect and safeguard the operating system disk and data disks at rest using industry standard encryption technology. The solution is integrated with Azure Key Vault to help customers manage the disk encryption keys and secrets in their Key Vault subscription and ensure that all data in the virtual machine disks is encrypted at rest in their Azure storage.

11. What is Azure Service Fabric for Windows Server?

Azure Service Fabric for Windows Server is a standalone runtime that lets customers create their own Service Fabric cluster on any set of Windows Server 2012 R2 or 2016 hosts, whether on-premises or in any cloud. This free download is now generally available with optional support provided through the purchase of an Azure support plan.

Azure Service Fabric now adds Linux as a choice of host operating system for Service Fabric cluster hosts. Linux hosts enable both Java and .NET applications running on Service Fabric

12. What is Storage Service Encryption for Azure Storage?

Azure Storage announces the general availability of Storage Service Encryption for Azure Blob storage (Block and Page Blobs) with any new Storage account created through Azure Resource Manager. Accounts enabled with this feature will have data encrypted with Microsoft-managed keys using the industry-leading encryption algorithm, 256-bit Advanced Encryption Standard (AES-256). Microsoft performs key management, rotation, and compliance with key standards.

13. What is Azure Premium Storage?

Azure Premium Storage is a solid-state drive (SSD)-based storage solution designed to support I/O-intensive workloads. With Premium Storage, you can add up to 64 TB of persistent storage per virtual machine, with more than 80,000 I/O Operations Per Second (IOPS) per virtual machine and extremely low latencies for read operations. It also offers a service-level agreement (SLA) for 99.9 percent availability.

What does automatic tuning boosts Azure SQL Database performance refer to?

A major update to Azure SQL Database Advisor greatly reduces the time required to produce and implement index-tuning recommendations. Now customers can run their production workload in SQL Database for a day, and Advisor will come up with relevant tuning recommendations to improve performance (and apply them when customers have enabled automated tuning).

14. What is an Azure Event Hubs Archive?

Customers can now automatically deliver streaming data in their event hubs into an Azure Blob storage account, with the ability to specify a time or size interval. Setting up Archive is quick. There are no administrative costs to run it and it scales automatically with Azure Event Hubs Throughput Units. Archive allows customers to focus on data processing rather than data capture. They can load data into Azure Data Lake, Azure Data Factory, and Azure HDInsight to perform batch processing and other analytics.

15. What are Azure Key Vault Certificates?

Azure Key Vault is introducing Key Vault Certificates to simplify tasks related to SSL/TLS certificates from supported third-party CAs. This enhancement helps customers enroll for certificates and automatically renew certificates while providing auditing trails within the same environment.

16. Why Microsoft Azure for IaaS?

- Many IT professionals have the skills to manage Microsoft products.
- Microsoft is a leader to provide end-to-end support when running Microsoft workloads.
- Integration with existing Microsoft products makes migration and hybrid configurations straightforward.
- Microsoft offers IaaS, PaaS, SaaS, and client operating systems with Windows and is a complete end-to-end solution.
- Microsoft is strong in both Cloud and Enterprise computing as well as analytics.

17. Is Azure Secure from a compliance perspective?

Azure meets a broad set of international and industry-specific compliance standards, such as ISO 27001, HIPAA, FedRAMP, SOC 1 and SOC 2, as well as country-specific standards like Australia IRAP, UK G-Cloud, and Singapore MTCS. Rigorous third-party audits, such as by the British Standards Institute, verify Azure's adherence to the strict security controls these standards mandate. As part of our commitment to transparency, you can verify our implementation of many security controls by requesting audit results from the certifying third parties.

18. What is usage typically measured and billed by in Azure?

- Hours
- Data Transfer (per GB)
- Storage (GB per month)
- Storage Transaction (per 10000)
- Virtual Machines/Instances
- Users

19. What are the different ways to pay for Azure?

- Pay as you go
- Microsoft Open License
- Enterprise Agreement
- MSDN subscription/partner benefit

20. How does one estimate costs with regard to infrastructure and usage in Azure?

The best way to estimate cost is to use Microsoft's Cost Estimator Tool which allows you to itemize all components you intend on using within the Azure realm.

21. What are some considerations for controlling your spending?

- Sizing and redundancy
- Which regions you intend on using
- Turning VM's on ar off
- Service or SLA choice
- Deconstruction or decommission of assets not in use.

22. What is an Azure SLA?

A Service Level Agreement (SLA) is provided for Azure services when Microsoft "guarantees" to meet a certain service level for a percentage of the time, often 99%.

23. What happens when Microsoft fails to meet its SLA?

A credit is provided for all services and time that violate the SLA.

24. What are the two types of Azure accounts used to moderate subscriptions and billing?

1. Microsoft accounts
2. Organizational accounts

25. What are the three primary ways Azure environments can be administered?

1. The Azure Web Portal
2. PowerShell
3. Programming Language API's

26. What web portals are available in Azure?

The classic or ASM (Azure Services Manager) and the new portal referred to as ARM (Azure Resource Manager).

27. Why would one use the classic portal vs the new portal?

Not all features and services are available in the classic web portal. Microsoft's intention is to migrate or deprecate the remcining features to the new portal as soon as possible.

28. What is the url to the classic web portal?

https://manage.windowsazure.com

29. What is the url to the new web portal?

https://portal.azure.com

30. In the new web portal, what does the term "Blade" refer to?

A blade shows information about a service or group of services. It is genera ly a panel of related information. Blades has a status bar at the top showing current status. They can be minimized, maximized, customized and pinned to the startboard. Blades car have command bars with tasks such as start and stop.

31. How do Blades show more detailed information?

- Quickstarts show tips and further documentation
- Settings give easy access to service configuration
- Monitoring parts show information about current and historical performance
- Tags enable an additional level of grouping and searching.

32. What is a "Journey" in the new web portal?

A Journey is a grouping of one or more blades.

33. What is an Azure Region?

Azure operates in multiple geographies around the world. An Azure geography is a defined area of the world that contains at least one Azure Region. An Azure region is an area within a geography containing one or more datacenters.

34. What is a paired Azure Region?

Each Azure region is paired with another region within the same geography, together making a regional pair. The exception is Brazil South which is paired with a region outside its geography. Microsoft recommends you replicate workloads across regional pairs to benefit from Azure's isolation and availability policies.

35. *What are examples of cross-region activities?*

- Azure Compute (PaaS) – You must provision additional compute resources in advance to ensure resources are available in another region during a disaster. For more information, see Azure resiliency technical guidance.
- Azure Storage - Geo-Redundant storage (GRS) is configured by default when an Azure Storage account is created. With GRS, your data is automatically replicated three times within the primary region, and three times in the paired region. For more information, see Azure Storage Recundancy Options.
- Azure SQL Databases – With Azure SQL Standard Geo-Replication, you can configure asynchronous replication of transactions to a paired region. With Premium Geo-replication, you can configure replication to any region in the world; however, we recommend you deploy these resources in a paired region for most disaster recovery scenarios. For more

information, see Geo-Replication in Azure SQL Database.

- Azure Resource Manager (ARM) - ARM inherently provides logical isolation of service management components across regions. This means logical failures in one region are less likely to impact another.

36. *What are some benefits of paired regions?*

- Physical isolation – When possible, Azure prefers at least 300 miles of separation between datacenters in a regional pair, although this isn't practical or possible in all geographies. Physical datacenter separation reduces the likelihood of natural disasters, civil unrest, power outages, or physical network outages affecting both regions at once. Isolation is subject to the constraints within the geography (geography size, power/network infrastructure availability, regulations, etc.).
- Platform-provided replication - Some services such as Geo-Redundant Storage provide automatic replication to the paired region.
- Region recovery order – In the event of a broad outage, recovery of one region is prioritized out of every pair. Applications that

are deployed across paired regions are guaranteed to have one of the regions recovered with priority. If an application is deployed across regions that are not paired, recovery may be delayed – in the worst case the chosen regions may be the last two to be recovered.

- Sequential updates – Planned Azure system updates are rolled out to paired regions sequentially (not at the same time) to minimize downtime, the effect of bugs, and logical failures in the rare event of a bad update.
- Data residency – A region resides within the same geography as its pair (with the exception of Brazil South) in order to meet data residency requirements for tax and law enforcement jurisdiction purposes.

37. What is Azure Automation?

Azure Automation is an Azure service that allows you to automate your management tasks and to orchestrate actions across external systems from right within Azure. It is built on PowerShell Workflow, so you can take advantage of the language's many features.

38. What is an Automation Runbook?

A Runbook is generally a PowerShell script of tasks that can take inputs and be run at scheduled times. They are part of Azure Automation.

39. What is Diagnostics in Windows Azure?

Windows Azure diagnostics provides facility to store diagnostics data. Some diagnostics data is stored in a table, while some is stored in a blob. For collecting diagnostics data, we must initialize the Windows Azure diagnostic monitor. The Windows Azure diagnostic monitor runs in Windows Azure and in the computer's emulator and collects diagnostic data for a role instance.

40. What is Azure Queue storage?

Azure Queue storage provides cloud messaging between application components. In designing applications for scale, application components are often decoupled, so that they can scale independently. Queue storage delivers asynchronous messaging for communication between application components, whether they are running in the cloud, on the desktop, on an on-premises server, or on a mobile device. Queue storage also supports managing asynchronous tasks and building process work flows.

Azure Queue storage is a service for storing large numbers of messages that can be accessed from anywhere in the world via authenticated calls using HTTP or HTTPS. A single queue message can be up to 64 KB in size, and a queue can contain millions of messages, up to the total capacity limit of a storage account.

41. *What are some common usages for Azure Queue?*

- Creating a backlog of work to process asynchronously
- Passing messages from an Azure web role to an Azure worker role

42. *What are Azure Storage Accounts?*

An Azure storage account provides a unique namespace to store and access your Azure Storage data objects. All objects in a storage account are billed together as a group. By default, the data in your account is available only to you, the account owner.

43. What are the two types of Azure Storage Accounts?

1. General-purpose Storage Accounts
2. Blob Storage Accounts

44. What are General-purpose Storage Accounts?

A general-purpose storage account gives you access to Azure Storage services such as Tables, Queues, Files, Blobs and Azure virtual machine disks under a single account.

45. What are Blob Storage Accounts?

A Blob storage account is a specialized storage account for storing your unstructured data as blobs (objects) in Azure Storage. Blob storage accounts are similar to your existing general-purpose storage accounts and share all the great durability, availability, scalability, and performance features that you use today including 100% API consistency for block blobs and append blobs. For applications requiring only block or append blob storage, we recommend using Blob storage accounts.

46. What are the two Access Tiers available for Blob storage?

1. A Hot access tier which indicates that the objects in the storage account will be more frequently accessed. This allows you to store data at a lower access cost.
2. A Cool access tier which indicates that the objects in the storage account will be less frequently accessed. This allows you to store data at a lower data storage cost.

47. How is Azure Storage usage billed?

You are billed for Azure Storage usage based on your storage account. Storage costs are based on the following factors: region/location, account type, storage capacity, replication scheme, storage transactions, and data egress (Not data ingress).

48. What are Storage Account endpoints?

Every object that you store in Azure Storage has a unique URL address. The storage account name forms the subdomain of that address. The combination of subdomain and domain name, which is specific to each service, forms an endpoint for your storage account.

For example, if your storage account is named "mystorageaccount", then the default endpoints for your storage account are:

Blob service:
http://mystorageaccount.blob.core.windows.net

Table service:
http://mystorageaccount.table.core.windows.net

Queue service:
http://mystorageaccount.queue.core.windows.net

File service:
http://mystorageaccount.file.core.windows.net

49. What is the primary difference between Azure Queues and Services Bus queues?

Simply put, Azure Queues, are part of the Azure storage infrastructure, featuring a simple REST-based Get/Put/Peek interface, providing reliable, persistent messaging within and between services.

Service Bus queues are part of a broader Azure messaging infrastructure that supports queuing as well as publish/subscribe, Web service remoting, and integration patterns.

While both queuing technologies exist concurrently, Azure Queues were introduced first, as a dedicated queue storage mechanism built on top of the Azure storage services. Service Bus queues are built on top of the broader "brokered messaging" infrastructure designed to integrate applications or application components that may span multiple communication protocols, data contracts, trust domains, and/or network environments.

50. *When is it advisable to use Azure Queues?*

- Your application must store over 80 GB of messages in a queue, where the messages have a lifetime shorter than 7 days.
- Your application wants to track progress for processing a message inside of the queue. This is useful if the worker processing a message crashes. A subsequent worker can then use that information to continue from where the prior worker left off.
- You require server side logs of all of the transactions executed against your queues.

51. *When is it advisable to use Service Bus Queues?*

- Your solution must be able to receive messages without having to poll the queue. With Service Bus, this can be achieved through the use of the long-polling receive operation using the TCP-based protocols that Service Bus supports.

- Your solution requires the queue to provide a guaranteed first-in-first-out (FIFO) ordered delivery.
- You want a symmetric experience in Azure and on Windows Server (private cloud). For more information, see Service Bus for Windows Server.
- Your solution must be able to support automatic duplicate detection.
- You want your application to process messages as parallel long-running streams (messages are associated with a stream using the SessionId property on the message). In this model, each node in the consuming application competes for streams, as opposed to messages. When a stream is given to a consuming node, the node can examine the state of the application stream state using transactions.
- Your solution requires transactional behavior and atomicity when sending or receiving multiple messages from a queue.
- The time-to-live (TTL) characteristic of the application-specific workload can exceed the 7-day period.

- Your application handles messages that can exceed 64 KB but will not likely approach the 256 KB limit.
- You deal with a requirement to provide a role-based access model to the queues, and different rights/permissions for senders and receivers.
- Your queue size will not grow larger than 80 GB.
- You want to use the AMQP 1.0 standards-based messaging protocol. For more information about AMQP, see Service Bus AMQP Overview.
- You can envision an eventual migration from queue-based point-to-point communication to a message exchange pattern that enables seamless integration of additional receivers (subscribers), each of which receives independent copies of either some or all messages sent to the queue. The latter refers to the publish/subscribe capability natively provided by Service Bus.
- Your messaging solution must be able to support the "At-Most-Once" delivery guarantee without the need for you to build the additional infrastructure components.
- You would like to be able to publish and consume batches of messages.

- You require full integration with the Windows Communication Foundation (WCF) communication stack in the .NET Framework.

52. What is an Azure Storage Table?

A Table is a type of Azure Storage where one can store data. Tables store data as collections of entities. An Entity has a primary key and a value. (Key-Value Pair)

53. What does Federation refer to in SQL Azure?

Federation is introduced in SQL Azure for scalability. Federation helps both administrators and developers to scale data. It helps administrators by making repartitioning and redistributing of data easier. It helps developers in the routing layer and sharding of data. It helps in routing without application downtime.

Federation does basic scaling of objects in a SQL Azure Database. Federations are the partitioned data. There can be multiple Federations within a database. And each Federation represents a different distribution scheme.

54. What is SQL Azure?

SQL Azure is the PaaS version of SQL Server. Microsoft SQL Services and Microsoft SQL Data Services are now known as Microsoft SQL Azure and SQL Azure Database. Microsoft Azure is the best way to use PAAS (Platform as a Service) where we can host multiple databases on the same Account. Microsoft SQL Azure has the same feature of SQL Server, i.e. high availability, scalability and security in the core.

55.   What is Windows Azure Traffic Manager?

Microsoft Azure Traffic Manager allows you to control the distribution of user traffic to your service endpoints running in different datacenters around the world.

Service endpoints supported by Traffic Manager include Azure VMs, Web Apps and cloud services. You can also use Traffic Manager with external, non-Azure endpoints.

Traffic Manager works by using the Domain Name System (DNS) to direct end-user requests to the most appropriate endpoint, based on the configured traffic-routing method and current view of endpoint health. Clients then connect to the appropriate service endpoint directly.

56. What is the difference between Azure Traffic Manager and Azure Load Balancer?

Azure Traffic Manager is DNS-level routing and balancing of traffic. It uses DNS responses to direct end-user traffic to globally distributed endpoints. Clients then connect to those endpoints directly.

Azure Load Balancer is Network-level routing and balancing. It works at the transport layer (Layer 4 in the OSI network reference stack). It provides network-level distribution of traffic across instances of an application running in the same Azure data center.

57. How are these different from an Application Gateway?

Application Gateway works at the application layer (Layer 7 in the OSI network reference stack). It acts as a reverse-proxy service, terminating the client connection and forwarding requests to back-end endpoints.

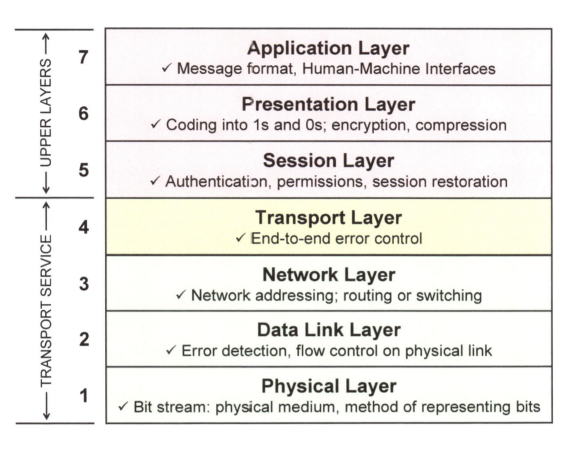

UPPER LAYERS	7	**Application Layer** ✓ Message format, Human-Machine Interfaces
	6	**Presentation Layer** ✓ Coding into 1s and 0s; encryption, compression
	5	**Session Layer** ✓ Authentication, permissions, session restoration
TRANSPORT SERVICE	4	**Transport Layer** ✓ End-to-end error control
	3	**Network Layer** ✓ Network addressing; routing or switching
	2	**Data Link Layer** ✓ Error detection, flow control on physical link
	1	**Physical Layer** ✓ Bit stream: physical medium, method of representing bits

58. *What are the three primary load-balancing methods used to distribute traffic in Azure Traffic Manager?*

1. Failover: Use this method when you want to use a primary endpoint for all traffic, but provide backups in case the primary becomes unavailable.

2. Performance: Use this method when you have endpoints in different geographic locations and you want requesting clients to use the

"closest" endpoint in terms of the lowest latency.

3. Round-Robin: Use this method when you want to distribute load across a set of cloud services in the same datacenter or across cloud services or websites in different datacenters.

59. What are the functions of Autoscaling Application Blocks?

Autoscaling Application Blocks can automatically scale the Windows Azure application based on the rules defined specifically for the application.

The Autoscaling Application Block supports two auto-scaling mechanisms:

1. Instance Autoscaling, where the block changes the number of role instances based on constraint and reactive rules.
2. Throttling, where the application modifies its own behavior to change its resource utilization based on a set of reactive rules. For example, switching off non-essential features, or gracefully degrading its UI.

60. What does profiling refer to in Azure?

Profiling is a process of measuring the performance analysis of an application. It is usually done to ensure that the application is stable enough and can sustain heavy traffic.

Visual Studio provides us various tools to do it by gathering the performcnce data from the application that also helps in the troubleshooting issues.

Once the profiling wizard is run, it establishes the performance session and collects the sampling data, then generates report files that can be opened and analyzed in Visual Studio.

61. What insights can profiling reports provide?

- Determine the longest running methods within the application.
- Measure the execution time of each method in the call stack.
- Evaluate memory allocation.
- Analyze concurrency issues (usually for multi-threaded code).

62. What is Service Fabric in Azure?

Service Fabric is a distributed systems platform that makes it easy to package, deploy, and manage scalable and reliable microservices. Service Fabric also addresses the significant challenges in developing and managing cloud applications. Developers and administrators can avoid solving complex infrastructure problems and focus instead on implementing mission-critical, demanding workloads knowing that they are scalable, reliable, and manageable. Service Fabric represents the next-generation middleware platform for building and managing these enterprise-class, Tier-1 cloud-scale applications.

63. What are two advantages to using microservices?

1. They enable you to scale different parts of your application depending on its needs.
2. Development teams are able to be more agile in rolling out changes and thus provide features to your customers faster and more frequently.

64. What are stateless Service Fabric microservices?

Stateless microservices (protocol gateways, web proxies, etc.) that do not maintain a mutable state outside of any given request and its response from the service.

65. What is the Azure Container Service?

The Azure Container Service makes it simpler for you to create, configure, and manage a cluster of virtual machines that are preconfigured to run containerized applications. It uses an optimized configuration of popular open-source scheduling and orchestration tools. Azure Container Service leverages the Docker container format to ensure that your application containers are fully portable.

66. What are Azure Cloud Services?

Cloud Services is an example of Platform-as-a-Service (PaaS). Like App Service, this technology is designed to support applications that are scalable, reliable, and cheap to operate. Just like an App Service is hosted on VMs, so too are Cloud Services, however, you have more control over the VMs. You can install your own software on Cloud Service VMs and you can remote into them.

67. *What are the two machine roles in a Cloud Service?*

1. Web role - Runs Windows Server with your web app automatically deployed to IIS.
2. Worker role - Runs Windows Server without IIS.

Ending notes

At this point you should be an interview god, or at least better off than when you started reading.

Remember, you shouldn't just memorize the answer without a thorough understanding of the concepts that lie behind the question and the answer. Hopefully this book has provided a decent review of what you already know or given you incentive to do additional research to gain better insight into the Cloud Computing field.

What did I miss?

If you feel like there are good questions you would like added or errata of any kind, please feel free to contact me and let me know. This book is meant to help everyone. The more helpful it is, the stronger we all are.